How to Start a Catering Business From Home

The Catering Playbook

By J. H. Dies

A Newbiz Playbook Publication

FIRST EDITION

ISBN 978-1539339892

For downloadable tools emailed directly to you please email **products@newbizplaybook.com** use the password Readytocater in the re: of the email

For my family, the answer to my why

Understanding Your "Product"

The fundamental truth about catering is that the product is, for those who hire you, a memory. Your task is to deliver a hassle free, great meal, well served. One of the biggest mistakes that new caterers make is to try to use low prices, or the perception of discounted value to attract customers. Your customers don't want the cheap option, and what's more they will be less likely to hire someone offering it.

People who hire professionals for this service are looking for a memorable experience. For you that means incredible preparation, and responsiveness. You provide a cell phone. You answer emails within hours if not minutes. For that, your customers will pay a premium. Your image, dress, tone, and interactions create this experience.

Nordstrom's is not an inexpensive store. Their products are expensive, even more expensive than other stores by a fair margin, but their client service and return policies are exceptional. The Ritz Carlton hosts very nice facilities, but honestly for the cost, they are not materially better than many less expensive hotels. The difference is in service, and the way they make their patrons feel.

Ignore this fundamental truth, and none of these contents will matter. Embrace it, and you will succeed. The goal is to create Raving Fans at every opportunity. The clients you help will have friends and family getting married, and you want them to insist on you to handle them.

Starting With a Plan

Many Caterers start their businesses from home with a dream to one day open and operate a restaurant, or even franchise a brand.

The business is a difficult one, and you should start with an idea of where you want to finish.

If you simply want to augment income, and have a talent for cooking, with no desire for anything more than a small and convenient home based business, your journey is easy.

If your goal is to grow to a food truck and/or a restaurant, you need to think about your brand.

Many caterers in the beginning will take whatever jobs they can get, cooking whatever they know how to make, and that is fine, but if your goal is a brand, you will want featured offerings that you have tested, that are well loved by your guests, and that you can deliver remotely without compromising product quality.

The ability to scale is also huge, because labor costs will dramatically impact margins and profitability.

How to Charge For Catering Services

A Huge Mistake New Caterers often make is failing to price their services for ALL costs.

You have overhead, costs of servers, time in shopping for, preparing, delivering, and serving the food. We will provide a pricing tool herein, but you should have a detailed breakout of all of your hard costs for internal purposes, and a presentation of key breakdown of your retail pricing for the client.

We have illustrated this with the Catering Proposal Template tool below:

Catering Proposal Template

Prepared for:
[Client.FirstName] [Client.LastName]
[Client.Company]
Prepared by:
[Sender.FirstName] [Sender.LastName]
[Sender.Client]

{Include thumbnail photos of your delicious food, branding information etc. If you have candid photos of people enjoying your food at a well decorated event those are nice as we

[Date Today]

Dear [Client.FirstName] [Client.LastName]:

[Sender.Company] is pleased to provide you with the attached catering proposal for your [Event Occasion], which is currently scheduled to be held on [Event Date] at [Event Location]. We understand that this is a very important occasion and we are committed to giving our utmost attention to make this a very memorable and stress free day.

In addition to an assortment of the finest foods and beverages, a knowledgeable and experienced staff, [Sender.Company] boasts a wide selection of china and silverware. Furthermore, we have strong relationships with the area's best vendors for any additional needs. Your dedicated event planner will work with you to design the best possible event which will reflect your own personal tastes and preferences. We are confident we can deliver all of these services while staying within your desired catering budget.

The attached proposal represents [Sender.Company]'s formal offer to provide catering services for the event described therein, upon the terms and conditions and pricing provided. As planning begins, some of the details in this document will change to suit your preferences and priorities. Consider this proposal an initial overview of our offerings in conjunction to your needs, and should you have any questions about the possibilities, please do not hesitate to contact me directly at [Sender.Email] or [Sender.Phone].

Thank you for the opportunity to provide you with this catering proposal. We very much look forward to the opportunity to work with you and to make this occasion a momentous one.

Sincerely,

ABOUT US

[Sender.Company] has been in business for [Number] years. We fulfill distinct event needs with excitement and creativity, the finest quality ingredients, and flawless elegance.

You name the celebration, describe the look and feel you are going for, and then relax. And relax some more. [Sender.Company] takes care of every detail of your memorable event.

With our unparalleled service, you can count on us to provide you with everything you need for your big event. When you hire [Sender.Company] you are guaranteed one of the best events you will ever attend.

GENERAL INFORMATION AND PARAMETERS

- Attendance – [Number of Guests] people (client Initials) _____
- Event Date – [Event Date] (client Initials) _____
- Event Location – [Event Location] (client Initials) _____
- Event Description – [Event Occasion] (client Initials) _____
- Budget – [Budget] (client Initials) _____

EQUIPMENT RENTALS

Equipment Needed	Price	QTY	Subtotal
Tent This is optional. In case of inclement weather, you may want to have your guests sheltered.	$500	1	$500
Dance floor Price is per square foot, quantity reflects the number of square feet needed.	$10	10	$100
Sound equipment	$500	1	$500

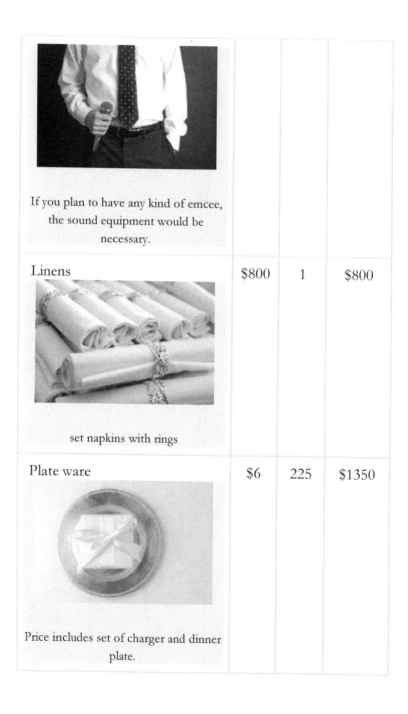

If you plan to have any kind of emcee, the sound equipment would be necessary.			
Linens set napkins with rings	$800	1	$800
Plate ware Price includes set of charger and dinner plate.	$6	225	$1350

Flatware Price includes standard 5 piece setting.	$4	225	$900
Stemware Price includes a water glass and wine glass.	$5	225	$1125

Tables and chairs 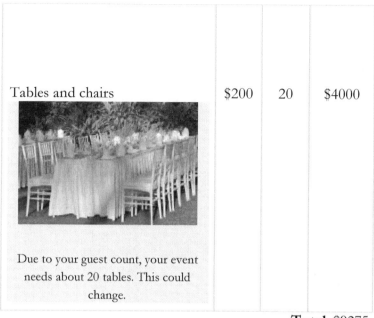 Due to your guest count, your event needs about 20 tables. This could change.	$200	20	$4000

Total: $9275

(client Initials) _____

MENU AND FOOD

1.   Appetizers – [Cost of Appetizers] per person
2.   Dinner – [Cost of Dinner Entree] per person
3.   Dessert – [Cost of Dessert] per person
4.   Drinks – [Cost of Drinks] per person

(client Initials)   _____

EVENT STAFF

We pride ourselves with providing you with the absolute best service. This includes ensuring the best staff will be on hand to make your event absolutely incredible. You can sit back and relax and let our professional servers, bartenders, and chefs take care of all the work.

Staff Member	No. of Staff Needed	Cost per Staff Member
Servers	[Number Servers to Guests]	[Cost per Server]

Bartenders	[Number Bartenders to Guests]	[Cost per Bartender]
Chefs	[Number Chefs to Guests]	[Cost per Chef]
Event Manager	[Number Mgrs to Guests]	[Cost per Event Manager]
Event Planner	[Number Planners to Guests]	[Cost per Event Planner]
Rental Equipment Delivery	2	Included

A designated event planner from [Event Planning Company] will also be provided and will serve as the main point of contact for [Client.Company].

(client Initials) _____

DECORATIONS

Centerpieces – pricing in accordance with [Event Planning Company] catalog available online at [Event Planning Website Address]

Flowers – pricing in accordance with [Event Planning Company] catalog available online at [Event Planning Website Address]

Lighting – pricing in accordance with [Event Lighting Company] catalog available online at [Event Lighting Website address]

Tables and Chairs – pricing in accordance with [Catering Company] catalog available online at [Catering Company Website Address]

(client Initials) _____

ENTERTAINMENT

- Band or DJ – from company
that [Client.Company] chooses. Contract will be separate
from any agreement with [Sender.Company]. Please let us
know if we can assist in helping you find the perfect
entertainment.

(client Initials)   _____

PRICING AND TERMS

Name of Service	Price
Food for Cocktail Hour and Reception	$13000
Table and Chair Rental	$5000
Plateware, Flatware, and Stemware	$2500

Subtotal: $20500

Sales tax (3%): $615

Total: $21115

A **50% deposit** will be due on or before **[Deposit Due Date]**. The **remaining balance** will be collected **a week prior** to the event. We accept all major credit cards and checks.

The estimated amount above is **not a fixed** amount and is **subject to change** based on actual charges and final guest counts and **any additional charges** approved by the Client.

_____   _____

Signature Client   Date

Catering Equipment Contract Template

CATERING AGREEMENT

This is a catering agreement {"Agreement"} executed this {date} day of {month}, {year},

BETWEEN

Client
{Address}
{Other Contact Info},
Referred to hereafter in this Agreement as "Client,"

AND

Your Business Name
{Address}
{Other Contact Info},
Referred to hereafter in this Agreement as "Caterer."

Client and Caterer agree to the following:

1. Services

1.1 Caterer agrees to provide food services to the Client for {basic description of event}, known as the "Event," taking place on {date}.

1.2 For this Event, Caterer agrees to provide the following: {detailed description}

1.3 Client agrees to provide the following: {is the client providing equipment, venue, chairs etc}

2. Deposit

2.1 Client is required to pay a deposit of _____ upon signing this Agreement. (1/3 to 50% is normal here)

2.2 This deposit is not refundable, as it will be used to acquire food and equipment from third parties which cannot be returned.

3. Payment

3.1 For the above services, Client will pay Caterer a total of {amount of money, This can be a set price for a certain menu, assuming a certain number of guests, or it can be a price per guest attending the event, or any other arrangement you agree to. Be specific, so that there are no hidden costs} , including the deposit outlined in Section 1.

3.2 If the Client should request additional food or services that will add to the total cost agreed upon by this contract, such must be agreed to in writing, either as an addendum to this Agreement, or in a separate document.

3.3. The balance on the total cost for the Event is due {at the end of Event, once all property has been returned to Client and/or Caterer, within 15 days of the Event, etc.}.

4. Guests

4.1 Client agrees to provide Caterer with the total number of guests no later than {number} days before Event.

4.2 Client agrees to break down the guest list into adults and children, and include any food allergies or special dietary requests, if applicable.

5. Menu

5.1 Client will {provide his/her own menu, choose from Caterer's available options, etc.}.

5.2 Menu must be confirmed by {length of time before the Event}, or else Client will be subjected to   {penalty fee amount}.

5.3 Menu will be fixed, and no changes may be made, {72 hours before Event, 24 hours before, etc.}.

6. Cancellation Policy

6.1 Client may cancel this Agreement {times when Client may cancel}.

6.2 Cancellation occurring {length of time} before Event will result in
{a total forfeiture of deposit, loss of 50% of deposit, etc.}, as
outlined in Section 2.

7. Arbitration

7.1 Should either party failure to provide or breach this Agreement in any way, the offending party will be liable for any damages.

7.2 Both parties agree to seek a third-party mediator or arbitrator for any disputes that arise as a result of this Agreement.

8. Jurisdiction

This Agreement falls under the jurisdiction of the state of {State}, and is therefore subject to all of {State's} laws and regulations.

Signed:

_____

Client Name

_____

Client Signature

_____

Caterer Name

_____

Caterer Signature

Date :_____

Equipment Considerations for Your Catering Business

Transportation:

> For most events a 15 passenger van with a row or two removed is a readily available, rentable vehicle that can be used to get large amounts of food to your venue efficiently. If you are using large heating cabinets, or have more food involved a box truck such as those available from U-Haul will do the trick.

> As your business grows, you may want a more custom vehicle with built in food warmers or refrigeration, but that should be down the road. Make sure rental costs or operation costs if you own are factored into your pricing

Kitchen Equipment:

> Many new caterers use the oven and refrigerator in their own kitchens for starting out. This requires planning from a capacity standpoint, so that everything that is not cooking is being kept warm, and are not in a situation where you can't get everything cooked in time.

> Kitchens can also be rented that have larger capacity. We recommend talking to your local church and rec center for the best prices. Larger more professional facilities can be more expensive. If your serving venue has its own kitchen, you may work in free access to use it as part of your total package at their facility, since you are bringing the venue business.

Portables:

> You should consider mobile equipment that can help you on site, once the food is prepared such as portable sinks, prep tables, and butane stoves. These can help you put finishing touches on your presentation on site to make the food look fantastic.

Food Transporting Equipment:

> You will need food carriers. They come in a number of sizes, and most are vinyl or plastic. They can hold as many as 24 food pans, and keep them warm or cold for hours. If you need a large number of them, you might consider also getting a dolly as they get quite heavy.

Mobile Beverage Dispensers:

> Even the simplest events have a couple of drink options, such as water, tea, or lemonade. A large dispenser that can carry 10 or so gallons is a very convenient and oft used piece of equipment.

Heating Cabinets.

> These can be expensive, but necessary, if you have a larger event, and they allow you to keep your food hot with either butane, or electric heat, which will improve your food quality.

Serving Equipment

> Buffet stands and risers will add to your presentation, and improve the formality of your event. This equipment can be rented at first, but if you are staying busy, it will be needed fairly quickly.

> Place settings, and china are also the responsibility of the caterer, unless alternate arrangements have been made. Rental companies can help here at first, but good looking, durable equipment will be needed by the business eventually.

Chairs and Tables

> These may be separately rented, but can be a source of revenue for your catering business, and they will pay for themselves quickly if you are able to stay busy. Many caterers rent these on the side for extra income.

Others

> You will need a utility cart for moving food from the kitchen or vehicle into the venue, and various other tasks.

You will need large mixing bowls, a good set of knives, and the equipment required to prepare your brand of food, which will vary quite a bit. As you prepare your menu (see menu tool below), you should be visualizing what equipment you have and what you need, to finish the job.

Where to Buy Equipment

In the beginning, we recommend that caterers look for quality used equipment in good shape that can be found at auctions, on craigslist, and on eBay and other websites. The value and savings are substantial, and many very established caterers will only buy used equipment.

Venue Checklist

This checklist is to be used for interviewing venues, and tracking their answers to insure that they are a good fit for the client's needs. It is always a good idea to tour the venue early where economics permit, to see for yourself if the place is as nice as the well situated online pictures make it appear to be. When a venue impresses you, be sure to document that, and keep it mind. Relationships with quality reliable vendors are absolutely essential to success in this business. Look for venues that can also help you build your business, and provide them with your menu offerings. If they help you with engagements, you should return the favor, and if you are bringing them business, let them know your expectations about getting help from them.

Capacity

     _____   Reception Area
     _____   Theatre/Meeting Room
     _____   Dining Area

Caterer

     _____   In-house tables/linens/chairs? If so, check out the quality.

     _____   How early can your caterer arrive day of event to set up?

Rental Fees

     _____   usually negotiable, especially for a major brand/off day
     _____   Does fee include a set up day?
     _____   how early/late can your teams load in?
     _____   any discount for payment by check or early payment?

Bathrooms

     _____   Will you need to provide extra amenities to make the room nicer

     _____   Cleanliness – poorly kept restrooms reflect poorly managed venue

     _____   Number of stalls vs. number of guests

Parking

     _____   Existent?

     _____   Fee to use parking lot?

     _____   Valets – included? Is there a preferred valet company?

     _____   Buses – if using buses - is there room to turn around, unload?

Shipments

     _____   Will the venue accept and store boxes a few days before event? $?

Audiovisual Team

     _____   Exclusive AV Company?

     _____   What tech operators are included, if any? (lighting tech, sound,   camera)

     _____   Cost of in-house AV Team/hour/operator

     _____   What AV exists in house? See the quality of the projector and check compatibility.

     _____   Internet Access- speed and logistics (do you need to drop lines, $$$)

     _____   Cost to use existing Internet lines

Stages

_____ Note any restrictions and size dimensions
_____ Height from ground to hang points
_____ See stage lighting with the room dark
_____ Existing backdrops, can you utilize these for event?
_____ If a stage must be brought in understand load-in logistics/restrictions

Registration/Place card area

_____ Is there a clean, open space near entrance of venue and in front of main room?
_____ How much signage can be placed outside of meeting room, in common areas?
_____ Will other events be held during meeting/wedding/party?
_____ Does venue have staff to help with registration/guiding guests to room?

Entrance

_____ Opportunity to brand/decorate entrance area?
_____ Curb appeal; are you comfortable with the current look/feel of the entrance?

Reception Area

_____ How close is the area to the ceremony/meeting room?
_____ Ideally a large open space with the ability to brand/decorate
_____ What furniture can be utilized for event?
_____ Will venue take away existing furniture you don't want for your   event?

Any charges?

_____ How early can you set up in this area?

Other Clients

_____ Who else has held events at this venue in recent
months?
_____ Testimonials? Can you contact references?
_____ Has a major competitor hosted parties at this
venue for a similar client base?

Electronic versions of this tool with room for notes are available
upon request at **products@newbizplaybook.com**.

Marketing for Caterers

Of all the challenges a new caterer faces, marketing the business can feel the most overwhelming. The good news is that you can very easily, and inexpensively market your business to a receptive target audience. The challenge will be follow through and consistency in maintaining exposure for your brand.

Whole books have been written on the subject of marketing, and this material is not designed to replace them. Our hope is to provide you with guidance as to how to spend your time, and where. You should understand the pros and cons of the various options out there, to make intelligent decisions on your ROI or return on investment. Everyone has different results with different media. As important as this is to your success, you should track where your leads (especially the ones that hire you), are coming from. Advertising that appears expensive at the outset, maybe cheap relative to other options when you see the revenue it is generating.

Website/SEO
Your website if properly done can be a very useful marketing tool, and may be one of the places you spend early money, once you start getting gigs. Wordpress.org, has some incredibly easy templated websites that can get you started. If you can get to a place where you are on the first or second page of google with your site, which is very doable, this will be the single most effective marketing vehicle you have. Keep in mind, you aren't looking to be first when someone types caterer." You are looking to be first when someone type "caterer in Cleveland." The difference between these two is what makes it vastly easier to rise to the top. I have, with no training whatsoever, been able to get several service based websites on the first page of google.

The key is to duplicate the search you want to be relevant for. For example, if the hope is that you come up first when someone types "great caterers in St. Louis," do that search, and then go to the sites on the first page and a half of google, and look at the content. You are specifically looking for whether there are videos or pictures, how often your key search term appears.

You are also looking for the titles used for the website's pages. For example if you click on a page, at the top right side of that page there will be a tab, with some language on it that is designed to summarize the content of that page. These are title tags, and this research on content, will tell you what you need to emulate to get to the top of google. Be careful. Copying text and directly duplicating material, or over using a few key words will get you punted from key word searches, which would kill the effectiveness of your website. When you start to book events, you should consider early investment in a great website with an SEO (search engine optimization) professional to help you.

We recommend that at a minimum, a third of all profits go back into the business to grow it and help with important investments in the business. This investment would be at the top of that list. If you have some resources already saved, this would boost visibility substantially and increase the speed with which your business gets noticed. There are a number of free-lance website development options out there. Do your research as this is a hugely important investment.

Sample Selling

Consider the local area, and businesses that might be in the market for your services, and take them samples! Even if the business doesn't hire you, if the people there love your food they may share your name or business cards with others who will hire you. This is a great, practical, and inexpensive way to get noticed. Try to feed the office managers who often make food purchasing decisions for the company.

Networking and Word of Mouth

Experienced, successful caterers will tell you that most of their new business comes from referrals and relationships they have formed with clients, and others in the business. This would include things like photographers, wedding planners, etc.

The challenge is to reach the level where the "machine" is sending you leads on a constant basis. As you build relationships with these professionals, and help them to build their businesses, it is reasonable to expect that they help with yours. You should be candid in hiring these folks about what you are looking for.

It is reasonable to demand promptness, professionalism, responsiveness, and elite service from these folks. Let them know that in your mind they are an extension of your brand, and if they provide an exceptional experience for your bride, you will help build their businesses. It is interesting to hear from new caterers that they feel uncomfortable asking these folks for referrals. That is part of the job here

In the beginning you should be very vocal to your personal network of friends and family to let them know you have begun to do this work, being sure to emphasize all of your efforts, research, and time spent getting to know the business.

Catering Open Houses

In advance of holidays, and peak catering times, open your house, or shop to guests, and have them come in and taste your best. Offer a menu that would complement holiday parties befitting the time of year, perhaps with a feature cocktail, and use the time they are tasting your wears to meet potential clients, and get their feedback on your food.

Wedding Shows

Wedding and Bridal Shows – Few venues will give you as much exposure to potential clients in such a short amount of time as Wedding shows. They are also among the most expensive marketing options available to a new startup. Prices for large city shows range from $1000 for a small booth to more than $1600 for a larger one. These costs don't include expenses for any attention getting show pieces you may want to feature. There will also be some competition among other planners vying for the business of the same clients in a relatively small setting. – Tip If you are just starting out, and don't have a good portfolio of pictures of your work (which we will talk about getting inexpensively or free from photographers later), research designs you like online with sites like Pinterest and others and create a book of "ideas we love for your weeding." Make sure these are things that you will be able to recreate with reasonable effort if asked to do so, but visualization is very important to getting clients to hire you.

Social Media

Social media is an incredibly effective and inexpensive means of advertising your business, and to a limited degree it is worth your time to learn how to get your brand up and running on Facebook, Instagram, twitter, Pinterest, and snapchat. This is how you build a following, and stay relevant to others who need to think of you first when they or someone they know decides to plan an event that requires catering. In the beginning these are free if not very inexpensive.

Ratings and specialty sites

There are a number of sites like Yelp, which allow businesses to put up very basic profiles for free. In the beginning, it can be helpful to put your site and business on as many of these as possible so that these sites point back to your website and business. When you sign up, you will be pitched on pay packages that help boost your chances of appearing early on these sites. In our experience these types of investment don't generate nearly as many live leads as search engine optimization. It is important to monitor these sites, and to regularly search for your site so that you can see what reviews are out there both good and bad, which could impact your business.

Phone books, mailers and other print advertising

We address these last, because frankly they are not very effective in generating revenue relative to the cost, at least in this business. At some point, you may be large enough to require a better add in a phone book, or need to have mail outs for clients to stay in front of them, but getting email addresses, and electronic communication is vastly more effective. We simply don't recommend spending startup dollars here.

You may have need for printed material in the form of business cards or trifolds, which can be handed out to guests who visit you at wedding shows etc. These are necessary expenditures, and when they are printed it should be high quality work on good card or paper stock. This stuff represents your brand, which must be elite if you want to command larger fees with your engagements.

We have included a great example of a tri fold in word form, so you don't have to play with formatting or make one yourself. Simply cut and paste photos or logos and add content as you see fit. Below is a printed example with two sides of a suggested layout, with content references that will allow you adjust the trifold to fit your business.

Food and Beverage Planning

One of the most important aspects of great catering is food and beverage planning. The best recipes in the world will not overcome the failure to bring or cook enough food. A party will suffer if the bar falls short. Similarly, clients will be angry if they feel they are charged for large amounts of wasted food or drinks. For this reason we have included a food and beverage planning tool, which should insure that you are in good shape on these matters.

Food and Drink Consumption Planning Tool

Appetizers

As you determine the appetizer quantity, consider what purpose the appetizers will serve. If you're serving appetizers before a main meal, you don't need as many as you do if the appetizers are the meal itself. Because appetizers are different from other food items, how much you need depends on several factors. Appetizers don't lend themselves to a quantity chart, per se, but let the following list guide you:

- For appetizers preceding a full meal, you should have at least four different types of appetizers and six to eight pieces (total) per person. For example, say you have 20 guests. In that case, you'd need at least 120 total appetizer pieces.

- For appetizers without a meal, you should have at least six different types of appetizers. You should also have 12 to 15 pieces (total) per person. For example, if you have 20 guests, you need at least 240 total appetizer pieces. This estimate is for a three-hour party. Longer parties require more appetizers.

- The more variety you have, the smaller portion size each type of appetizer will need to have. Therefore, you don't need to make as much of any one particular appetizer.

- When you serve appetizers to a crowd, always include bulk-type appetizers. Bulk-type foods are items that aren't individually made, such as dips or spreads. If you forgo the dips and spreads, you'll end up making hundreds of individual appetizer items, which may push you over the edge. To calculate bulk items, assume 1 ounce equals 1 piece.

- Always try to have extra items, such as black and green olives and nuts, for extra filler.

When appetizers precede the meal, you should serve dinner within an hour. If more than an hour will pass before the meal, then you need to increase the number of appetizers. Once again, always err on the side of having too much rather than too little.

Quantity planning for soups, sides, main courses, and desserts

The following tables can help you determine how much food you need for some typical soups, sides, main courses, and desserts. If the item you're serving isn't listed here, you can probably find an item in the same food group to guide you.

You may notice a bit of a discrepancy between the serving per person and the crowd servings. The per-person serving is based on a plated affair (where someone else has placed the food on the plates and the plates are served to the guests). In contrast, buffet-style affairs typically figure at a lower serving per person because buffets typically feature more side dish items than a plated meal does. Don't use the quantity tables as an exact science; use them to guide you and help you make decisions for your particular crowd. If you're serving a dish that you know everyone loves, then make more than the table suggests. If you have a dish that isn't as popular, you can get by with less.

Soups and Stews

Soup or Stew	Per Person	Crowd of 25	Crowd of 50
Served as a first course	1 cup	5 quarts	2-1/2 gallons
Served as an entree	1-1/2 to 2 cups	2 to 2-1/2 gallons	4 gallons

Main Courses

Entree	Per Person	Crowd of 25	Crowd of 50
Baby-back ribs, pork spareribs, beef short ribs	1 pound	25 pounds	50 pounds
Casserole	N/A	Two or three 9-x-13-inch casseroles	Four or five 9-x-13-inch casseroles
Chicken, turkey, or duck (boneless)	1/2 pound	13 pounds	25 pounds
Chicken or turkey (with bones)	3/4 to 1 pound	19 pounds	38 pounds
Chili, stew, stroganoff, and other chopped meats	5 to 6 ounces	8 pounds	15 pounds
Ground beef	1/2 pound	13 pounds	25 pounds
Maine lobster (about 2 lbs. each)	1	25	50
Oysters, clams, and mussels (medium to large)	6 to 10 pieces	100 to 160 pieces	200 to 260 pieces
Pasta	4 to 5 ounces	7 pounds	16 pounds
Pork	14 ounces	22 pounds	44 pounds
Roast (with bone)	14 to 16 ounces	22 to 25 pounds	47 to 50 pounds

Roast cuts (boneless)	1/2 pound	13 pounds	25 pounds
Shrimp (large: 16 to 20 per pound)	5 to 7 shrimp	7 pounds	14 pounds
Steak cuts (T-bone, porterhouse, rib-eye)	16 to 24 ounces	16 to 24 ounces per person	16 to 24 ounces per person
Turkey (whole)	1 pound	25 pounds	50 pounds

Side Dishes

Side Dish	Per Person	Crowd of 25	Crowd of 50
Asparagus, carrots, cauliflower, broccoli, green beans, corn kernels, peas, black-eyed peas, and so on	3 to 4 ounces	4 pounds	8 pounds
Corn on the cob (broken in halves when serving buffet-style)	1 ear	20 ears	45 ears
Pasta (cooked)	2 to 3 ounces	3-1/2 pounds	7 pounds
Potatoes and yams	1 (medium)	6 pounds	12 pounds
Rice and grains (cooked)	1-1/2 ounces	2-1/2 pounds	5 pounds

Side Salads

Ingredient	Per Person	Crowd of 25	Crowd of 50
Croutons (medium size)	N/A	2 cups	4 cups
Dressing (served on the side)	N/A	4 cups	8 cups
Fruit salad	N/A	3 quarts	6 quarts
Lettuce (iceberg or romaine)	N/A	4 heads	8 heads
Lettuce (butter or red leaf)	N/A	6 heads	12 heads
Potato or macaroni salad	N/A	8 pounds	16 pounds
Shredded cabbage for coleslaw	N/A	6 to 8 cups (about 1 large head of cabbage)	12 to 16 cups (about 2 large heads of cabbage)
Vegetables (such as tomato and cucumber)	N/A	3 cups	6 cups

Breads

Bread	Per Person	Crowd of 25	Crowd of 50
Croissants or muffins	1-1/2 per person	3-1/2 dozen	7 dozen
Dinner rolls	1-1/2 per person	3-1/2 dozen	7 dozen
French or Italian bread	N/A	Two 18-inch loaves	Four 18-inch loaves

Desserts

Dessert	Per Person	Crowd of 25	Crowd of 50
Brownies or bars	1 to 2 per person	2-1/2 to 3 dozen	5-1/2 to 6 dozen
Cheesecake	2-inch wedge	Two 9-inch cheesecakes	Four 9-inch cheesecakes
Cobbler	1 cup	Two 9-x-9-x-2-inch pans	Four 9-x-9-x-2-inch pans
Cookies	2 to 3	3 to 4 dozen	6 to 8 dozen
Ice cream or sorbet	8 ounces	1 gallon	2 gallons
Layered cake or angel food cake	1 slice	Two 8-inch cakes	Four 8-inch cakes
Pie	3-inch wedge	Two or three 9-inch pies	Four or five 9-inch pies
Pudding, trifles, custards, and the like	1 cup	1 gallon	2 gallons
Sheet cake	2-x-2-inch piece	1/4 sheet cake	1/2 sheet cake

Alcohol and Beverage Planning

Concerning drinks, let the following list guide you:

Soft drinks: One to two 8-ounce servings per person per hour.

Punch: One to two 4-ounce servings per person per hour.

Tea: One to two 8-ounce servings per person per hour.

Coffee: One to two 4-ounce servings per person per hour.

Water: Always provide it. Two standard serving pitchers per table are usually enough.

Again, err on the side of having too much. If people are eating a lot and having fun, they tend to consume more liquid.

Alcohol Consumption and Pricing Projection Tool

There is always some subjectivity in alcohol planning. The assumption here is that 75% of the guests are drinking alcohol. This should be discussed, as a higher percentage of children in attendance, a group of heavier drinkers etc., could impact these assumptions.

As always we recommend adding 10% to all estimates. You will frustrate guests if there is insufficient alcohol, so make sure they are in agreement with your assumptions on numbers. They will know their guests better than anyone. The cost estimates assume average costs on beer, wine, and liquor. Premium beer, wine, and liquor would also mean increased costs. This also assumes equal consumption i.e. 25% each of beer, wine, and liquor. Beer drinkers tend to range closer to 40%, but these figures make scaling for your needs much easier.

The following should help plan for reception alcohol consumption. BD = beer drinker, WD = wine drinker, LD = liquor drinker

	Small Wedding (100 guests)	
	Amount	Cost
Beer	5 cases per 25 BD	75.00
Wine	20 bottles per 25 WD	160.00
Liquor	6 750 ml bottles per 25 LD	90.00

	Medium Wedding (200 guests)	
	Amount	Cost
Beer	9 cases per 50 BD	135.00
Wine	40 bottles per 50 WD	320.00
Liquor	12 750 ml bottles per 50 LD	180.00

	Large Wedding (100)	
	Amount	Cost
Beer	3 Kegs 100 BD	270.00
Wine	79 bottles per 100 WD	632.00
Liquor	24 750 ml bottles per 100 LD	360.00

Electronic versions of this spreadsheet are available upon request at **products@newbizplaybook.com**.

Menu Card Template

COMPANY or EVENT LOGO

(print logo in color for more effect)

August 16, 2016

Appetizer

Heirloom Tomatoes Tower

with Organic Farms Goat Ricotta

Salad

Endive & Spring Vegetable Salad

with Fava Beans, Confit Cherry Tomatoes & Baby
Asparagus

Entrée

Pan Roasted Alaskan Halibut

with Caramelized Corn & Wild Chanterelle Mushrooms

or

Grilled Prime Bone-In New York Steak

Peppercorn Sauce & Sautéed Fingerling Potatoes

Dessert

Chocolate Tres Leche Cake

Espresso-truffle Ice Cream, Kahlua Crème Chantilly

Square Shaped Menu Card Template

COMPANY or EVENT LOGO
August 16, 2008

Appetizer
Heirloom Tomatoes Tower
with Organic Farms Goat Ricotta

Salad
Endive & Spring Vegetable Salad
with Fava Beans, Confit Cherry Tomatoes & Baby Asparagus

Entrée
Pan Roasted Alaskan Halibut
with Caramelized Corn & Wild Chanterelle Mushrooms
or
Grilled Prime Bone-In New York Steak
Peppercorn Sauce & Sautéed Fingerling Potatoes

Dessert
Chocolate Tres Leche Cake
Espresso-truffle Ice Cream, Kahlua Crème Chantilly

Linen Planning Tool

TABLE SIZE	SEATS	54" Sq	80" Sq	90" Sq	72x120"	70x170"	90x132"	90x156"	96" Rnd	108" Rnd	120" Rnd	126" Rnd	132" Rnd
4x30"	4	Overlay	16x28" Drop										
6x30"	6-8			Overlay	24x27 Drop	Box	To Floor All Sides		Overlay, Pinned	Overlay, Pinned	Overlay, Pinned		
8x30"	8-10			Overlay	12x27 Drop	Box		To Floor All Sides	Overlay, Pinned	Overlay, Pinned	Overlay, Pinned		
6x18"	3 (One Side)				24x27 Drop	Box							
8x18"	4 (One Side)				12x27 Drop	Box							
30"x30"	4	12" Drop*	28" Drop*	To Floor All Sides									

TABLE SIZE	SEATS	54" Sq	80" Sq	90" Sq	72x120"	70x170"	90x132"	90x156"	96" Rnd	108" Rnd	120" Rnd	126" Rnd	132" Rnd
30" Round	3	Overlay 12" Drop							To Floor				
3' Round	4	Overlay 9" Drop	Overlay 22" Drop*						To Floor				
Cafe Table	Standing	Overlay 9" Drop	Overlay 22" Drop*	Overlay 27" Drop					Overlay 30" Drop		To Floor		
4' Round	6	Overlay 9" Drop	Overlay 16" Drop*	Overlay 21" Drop					Overlay 24" Drop	To Floor			
5' Round	8-10	Overlay Top	Overlay 10" Drop*	Overlay 18" Drop					Overlay 18" Drop	Overlay 24" Drop	To Floor		
5½' Round	9-10		Overlay 7" Drop*	Overlay 12" Drop					Overlay 15" Drop	Overlay 21" Drop	Overlay 27" Drop	To Floor	
6' Round	10-12		Overlay Top	Overlay 9" Drop					Overlay 12" Drop	Overlay 18" Drop	Overlay 24" Drop	Overlay 27" Drop	To Floor
72" Round											1 Cloth, Folded		
Serpentine	Buffet	3 Cloths with 2 Skirts			1 Cloth with 2 Skirts	1 Cloth							

Banquet Table

Table Size	Seating Capacity	Linen Size	Space Needed
6'	6-8	90" x 132"	11" x 7"
8'	8-10	90" x 156"	13' x 7'
Classroom 6'	4	70" x 170"	11' x 6'
Classroom 8'	6	70" x 170"	13' x 6'

Round Table

Cocktail Table

Table Size	Seating Capacity	Linen Size	Space Needed
2.5'	2-4	96" round	7' diameter
3'	4-5	96" round	8' diameter
4'	6-8	108" round	9' diameter
5'	8-10	120" round	10' diameter
6'	10-12	132" round	11' diameter

Table Size	Seating Capacity	Linen Size	Space Needed
2.5'	2-4	108" round	7' diameter
3'	4-5	120" round	8' diameter

Catering Planner Contact Tool

Communication must be exceptional to insure repeat business. We recommend that you keep a specific contacts page for each of your events. Larger caterers

Event Details

Event Date _____

Client Contact Name _____

Phone _____ email _____

Client Address _____

City _____ Zip _____

Venue Name _____

Venue Address _____

City _____ Zip _____

Rec Venue Address _____

City _____ Zip _____

Photographer _____

Photographer Phone _____

Videographer _____

Videographer Phone _____

Caterer _____

Caterer Phone _____

Electronic versions of this spreadsheet are available upon request at products@newbizplaybook.com.

DJ style preference (active vs. camouflage)

Order of Events (please number 1-15)

Introduction	Toast	Father Daughter
Blessing	First Dance	Mother Groom
Bouquet Toss	Last Dance	Cake Cutting
Garter Toss	Other	Other
Other	Other	Other

Dinner Music or Special Songs

1._____ 2._____

3._____ 4._____

5._____ 6._____

7._____ 8._____

9._____ 10._____

11._____ 12._____

Electronic versions of this spreadsheet are available upon request at **products@newbizplaybook.com**.

Dance Floor Planning Tool

This tool has been designed to allow you to plan and scale necessary floor space for dancing. For parties greater than 250, simply use multiples of the tables below. If more than 50% of guests are expected to be dancing, ignore the guests invited column, and plan based upon the number of dancers in the second column.

Total Guests	Dancers	Dance FL Size	Floor SQ Feet
24	12	8'x8'	64
36	18	8'x12'	96
48	24	8'x16'	128
64	32	12'x12'	144
72	36	12'x16'	192
90	45	12'x20	240
96	48	16'x16'	256
120	60	16'x24'	384
128	64	16'x24'	384
144	72	16'x24'	384
150	75	20'x20'	400
168	84	16'x28'	448
180	90	20'x24'	480
192	96	16'x32'	512
210	105	20'x28'	560
250	125	24'x28'	672

Guest List Management Tool

This tool is most easily used in spreadsheet form. An excel file tool is available at newbizplaybook.com. For those who want to download it.

With proper planning, a fair amount of information is needed on each guest including:

1. First and last name

2. Telephone number

3. Address and/or email address

4. Invitation sent

5. Confirmed for attending wedding/or not

6. Confirmed for attending pre-wedding dinner/or not – out of town guests for example

7. Wedding gift

8. Thank you letter sent

Download a great tool for helping the bride and groom keep track of attendance, and their responsibilities for thank you cards etc. This tool also helps the event planner to track and make adjustments for food, dance etc., in the event that more or fewer guests attend than expected. Electronic versions of this spreadsheet will be sent to readers upon request at **products@newbizplaybook.com**.

Important People Contact List

This tool is related, but different. Catering and event planners need to have visibility, and to some degree information about the VIP guests. Whoever is hiring you to plan their event wants the people dearest to them to enjoy it as much as possible. For you to build that robust referral network that will grow your business, you need to see to these folks.

For the VIP guests, you will want to know:

1. Full name

2. Relationship to the client

3. Cell phone if assisting with arrangements

4. Flight information if planner will be assisting with transportation (arrivals departures etc.)

5. Hotel details

6. Notes if needed.

We have a spreadsheet tool that will help to track these issues at **products@newbizplaybook.com**.

Co Vendor Contact Planning Sheet

Vendor	Business Name	Contact Name	Contact Number	Payment Status
Photographer				
Minister/Rabi				
Bakery				
Bar Tenders				
Wait staff				
Caterer				
Videographer				
D.J.				
Flowers				

Vendor Commitment Sheet

Vendor	Commitment	Arrival Time	Notes -	Gets Meal -
Photographer	8 hours x2			
Minister/Rabi				
Bakery		2.pm		
Bar Tenders				
Wait staff				No
Caterer				
Videographer				
D.J.				
Flowers				

Invoice Template

Your invoice is as much a reflection of your brand as any business card. You want to finish your engagement as professionally as you started it. We have included a template, and an electronic copy is available at **products@newbizplaybook.com**. Your invoice should include all of the following:

[Company Name]
[Company slogan]

INVOICE

[Street Address]
[City, ST ZIP Code]
Phone [Phone] | Fax [Fax]
[Email] | [Website]

INVOICE # [Invoice No.]
DATE [Date]

TO
[Name]
[Company Name]
[Street Address]
[City, ST ZIP Code]
Phone [Phone] | [Email]

FOR [Project or service description]
P.O. # [P.O. #]

Description	Amount

Total

Make all checks payable to [Company Name]
Payment is due within 30 days.
If you have any questions concerning this invoice, contact [Name] | [Phone] | [Email]

THANK YOU FOR YOUR BUSINESS!

Photographer Interview Questions

If you are going to bring in other vendors, you should be able to insure that they are qualified to serve your clients. Attached are some questions to ask when interviewing photographers, but prior to that, you should speak to your client about what they want in terms of wedding photography both in the deliverable, and with the style of photographer and his interaction with guests, and the wedding party. The photographer should be willing to answer these questions and this interview will give you a sense of his or her business temperament. Eventually you will have a stable of talented vendors who can help you here based on your specific needs, and you may develop special requests that help you make the events you handle unique. *You should also be prepared to provide the photographer with any needed information such as divorced guests, who do not wish to be photographed together etc.

1. Do you have my date available?

2. Do you have an online portfolio that I, and/or my client can review to get a sense of your style, and how recent is the material on it?

3. How far in advance do I need to book with you?

4. How long have you been in business/How many weddings have you shot?

5. Are there references you can offer from prior clients or planners? Note: This is the important question in the interview. Do not hire someone who cannot provide you this information, and call at least a couple of the references to compare their answers to your photographer's responses to these questions.

6. How would you describe your photography style (e.g. traditional, photojournalistic, and creative)?

7. How would you describe your approach to interacting with wedding party and guests, i.e. blending in, stirring the pot for creative photos, choreographing shots?

8. What type of equipment do you use?
9. Are you shooting in digital or film format or both?

10. Do you shoot in color and black & white?

11. Can I give you a list of specific shots we would like?

12. How will you (and your assistants) be dressed?

13. Is it okay if other people take photos while you're taking photos?

14. Have you ever shot at (wedding/reception venue)? If not, would you be willing to visit in advance to plan?

15. What time will you arrive at the site and for how long will you shoot?

16. If my event lasts longer than expected, will you stay? Is there an additional charge?

17. Can you put together a slideshow of the bride and groom with provided photos and/or a real time slide show for viewing at the reception?

18. What information do you need from me before the wedding day?

19. What is your rate, and how is ownership of the photos handled? Bride and groom may want to own the photos to copy and use as they see fit, and this may impact price.

20. Are you the photographer who will shoot my wedding? If not, who will shoot it, and can I see their work? If so, who will be assisting you and how?

21. What are your travel charges/requirements if any?

22. Are you photographing other events on the same day as this event?

23. What type of album designs do you offer? Do you provide any assistance in creating an album?

24. Do you provide retouching, color adjustment or other corrective services?

25. How long after the wedding will I get the proofs? Will they be viewable online? On a CD?

26. What is the ordering process?

27. How long after I order my photos/album will I get them?

28. Will you give me the negatives or the digital images, and is there a fee for that?

29. When will I receive a written contract?

30. What is your refund/cancellation policy? Do you have someone who covers your events in case of emergency or equipment failure?

Florist Interview Questions

1. Do you have my date available?

2. Do you have an online portfolio that I, and/or my client can review to get a sense of your style, and how recent is the material on it?

3. How far in advance do I need to book with you?

4. How long have you been in business/How many weddings have you handled?

5. Are there references you can offer from prior clients or planners? Note: This is the important question in the interview. Do not hire someone who cannot provide you this information, and call at least a couple of the references to compare their answers to your photographer's responses to these questions.

6. Given the size of this wedding, flower preference, color scheme, and venue specifics for church and reception, what would you propose? Note: Do not lead with your budget. Advise that you are open and want to see the proposal for a few different packages, so that you can compare costs.

7. What time will you arrive at the site and how long will it take you to set up?

8. Who will be managing the setup?

9. Are you providing flowers for other events on the same day as this event?

10. Any rental fees for vases or decorations the florist is providing?

11. Any additional labor charges, taxes, or other fee?

12. When will I receive a written contract?

13. What is your refund/cancellation policy? Do you have someone who covers your events in case of emergency? Note: It is common to require a 50% down payment.

Other Event Planning Tools

When we put this book together, we received a ton of great feedback from caterers all over the event community, and one of the first comments they had was, "Can you add a section for (Bar mitzvah, Quincinera, or other large events/conferences)?" The following tools were born of our desired interest in helping readers, and in hopes of helping to increase the flexibility of their service offerings.

Bar/Bat Mitzvah Reception Tool

Contact Information

Client name: Phone/Email:

Bar (boy) / Bat (girl) *(circle one)* Mitzvah name:

Reception Date:.   Setup Start Time:

Entertainment Start Time: End Time:

The following is a typical but optional sequence of events. The specifics should be coordinated with relevant venders such as caterers, and DJ's etc.

Sequence	Time	Event
		Guests Arrive
		Cocktail Hour
		Main Reception Starts (guests join each other in main hall)
		Family Entrance
		Candle Lighting
		Hora
		Kiddush
		Motzi
		Toasts
		Salad within 30 minutes of entrance
		Guest of Honor/Parent Dance
		Main Course
		Host/Hostess Dance
		Dessert
		Open Dancing
		Finale

Venue Information

There are other tools in this publication for helping you to interview, plan for, and qualify the venue for your event. Those may be used here, so for example, there is a guest tracker in the wedding section. You may want to use something different for this event, but that will work here.

Name/address of establishment:

Contact name: Phone:

Primary room name/location:

Planning Logistics

Number of guests: Children:

Day School Guest of Honor attends: Hebrew School Guest of Honor attends:

Party Theme:

Number of courses to be served (including dessert):

Will the caterer be using the dance floor for a buffet during the cocktail hour?   During the main course?

Contact Information for Other Party Professionals

	Name	Phone	email	Booked From_ to _
Wedding Planner	Kathy's Weddings	(123)456-789	abc@def.com	7-9:30
Banquet Hall/Venue				
Planner/Coordinator				
Photographer				
Videographer				
Entertainer				

Customer Tracking Tool

Customer Name	Phone	Email	Address	Last Contacted	Last Ordered	Notes

Event Wrap Closeout Tool

As a caterer, it is very important to close out your events with detailed information you can use for future reference in the event you seek to use the facility for future events.

Name of Event:
Date:
Chair/Event Producer: Your name or the event chair
Executive Host: sr. exec that served as the internal champion
Location: name of venue, city, state

BUDGET
Event Budget: Total allotted event budget
Actual Budget: $
Any Major Overruns & Reason: good to know
Outstanding Payments/Issues: list any disputes, outstanding major bills that may be en route, hopefully this is blank

EVENT STAFF

Number for Event: 14 onsite staff members, 6 were from J&J Temps

Number recommended for next year: Example: We would benefit from four more hosts at the golf tournament check in and a few more during the cocktail party registration desk.

Quotes from Clients/Attendees:
Share some great testimonials here received verbally or via email post event that your team, execs or future planners would enjoy hearing.

Final recommendations for next event:

Photos:
Add a few photos of the event that help jog your memory the next time around or help the next person. Centerpieces, signage, registration tables and stage sets are great to keep on file.

Staffing and Planning Tool

You will need to have planned your assistance very well to make sure you are not spending too much on staff, and to insure that your guests are properly served. In the beginning you will be using folks you know on an occasional basis, or hiring temps through a hospitality company in your city. As your business grows, you will better be able to plan whether it makes sense to hire employees.

The following is a tool that will help you work through how much help you may need. We recommend adding 10% or 1 person, whichever is more, to your staffing recommendations.

Buffet Style

You will need 2 folks for first 30 or so guests for service, presentation and takedown. Two additional runners or all purposes assistants are required for every 160 guests. More staff may be required if you have carving stations etc.
Other Examples:

Seated Dinners

You will need a server per every two 8-12 guest tables to help with clearing food and plates, and service of wine etc. You should also have a water/tea server to help with overflow for every four such tables.

Bartenders

We recommend a bartender for every 25 or so adult guests. If you have a more complex bar offering and a full service mixed drink menu, this may need to be adjusted accordingly.

Food Truck Section

We have had a ton of clients ask us about how to take their business to the next level with a food truck. We are here to help! We built this section to give you a launching point that can help you get your catering business out of your home, and onto the road.

Food Truck Startup Spreadsheet

Equipment	Estimated Cost	Notes
This will be cost for the vehicle, any external decorations or wrap, and the interior restaurant equipment such as grills, refrigerators, food storage and cabinets etc. We recommend as much stainless steel as you can afford. We have a tool herein with some vendors	$30,000 - $80,000	You can find less expensive trucks that are used, or that have less features, but if you are buying a used truck, have a mechanic inspect thoroughly
Initial Product Inventory - food and beverages	$1,000 - $2,000	
Permits and Licenses	$100 - $500	Different cities have vary, and some may require that you take sanitation, or food service classes to get certified by the city
Website	Free - $2,500	Your most important marketing other than word of mouth. Don't get cheap here.
Cash Register/point of sale for credit cards	$200 - $1,000	Phones and tablets using square or other credit transaction apps will be helpful in the beginning
Uniforms / T-Shirts	$0 - $1,000	Part of your branding
Paper Products (Cups/Plates / Napkins, etc.)	$200 - $300	
Misc. Expenses (Like a Chalk Menu)	$500 - $2000	Plan for some unexpected expenses here and put it into the budget.
Smallwares: Pots, Pans, etc.	$1000 - $2000	
Fire Extinguisher	$100 - $300	
Total Low End	$33,300	
Total High End	$91,600	

Food Truck Operations Spreadsheet

Item	Monthly Estimated Cost	Notes
Parking or Host Charges	varies	You may have to pay for a stall, or pay a business a percentage of revenue to offer products to their employees
Phone / Internet	$100 - $200	
Fuel	$500	This will vary a lot.
Labor	8-15 dollars per hour	$8 - $15 per hour is average rate.
Repairs	$1,000	Just for protection
Food / Beverage Restock	varies based upon sales expect to replenish food stocks weekly, obviously if you have a great weekend, it may happen more often	
Paper Product Restock	$800-$1600	Depends on food cost and frequency of operation.
Insurance	$50 - $150	Depends on food cost and frequency of operation.
Total:		

Great Sites for Food Trucks

http://www.buyfoodtruck.net/

http://www.cateringtruck.com/

http://apexspecialtyvehicles.com/

http://www.onthemovetrucks.com/otm-food-trucks

http://www.mr-trailers.com/

http://www.customconcessionsusa.com/

http://www.detroitcustomcoach.com/

https://northwestmobilekitchens.com/

http://www.bostonianbody.com/default.html

http://www.sybbq.com/

http://doublertrailers.com/

https://snoshack.com/

http://mobilekitchensolutions.net/contact-us/

Sample Buffet Illustration Tool

Prepare a drawing or layout of your table and service configuration in advance of your event. This can be easily done with Microsoft Word, and will give clarity to your assistants on the vision you have for food service. A detailed example is below, but you needn't be this specific.

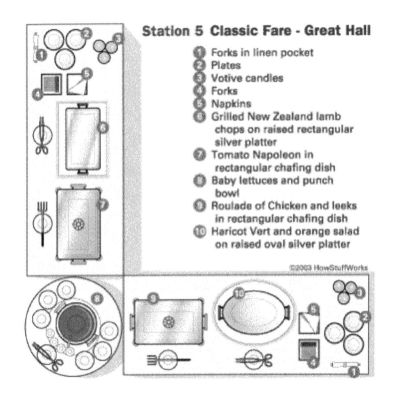

Station 5 Classic Fare - Great Hall

1. Forks in linen pocket
2. Plates
3. Votive candles
4. Forks
5. Napkins
6. Grilled New Zealand lamb chops on raised rectangular silver platter
7. Tomato Napoleon in rectangular chafing dish
8. Baby lettuces and punch bowl
9. Roulade of Chicken and leeks in rectangular chafing dish
10. Haricot Vert and orange salad on raised oval silver platter

©2003 HowStuffWorks

Proper Table Setting Design Configurations Tool

The following is designed to ensure that you offer your guests proper plates, flatware, and glassware in every combination. With multiple course meals, be sure to plan for extra plates and flatware, as this may be changed out during the dining experience. For purpose of these examples we have assumed water and tea for beverage service. Wine service is depicted below. This should be cumulative, i.e. if you are serving more than one of the below, be sure to add the relevant flatware. (we have included an example at the end)

Oyster or Cocktail configuration. (For Appetizer)

Salad Plating Configuration

Bread Service Configuration

Soup Service Configuration

Fish/Meat Service Configuration

Desert Properly Served with Fork Configuration

Desert Properly Served with Spoon Configuration

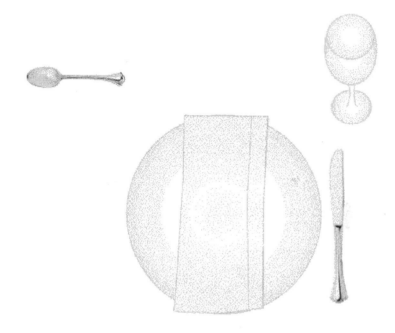

Red or White Wine Service Configuration (Note wine glass is positioned in the upper diagonal relative to the water or tea glass)

Coffee Service Configuration

Complete Meal (Shrimp Cocktail, Bread, Salad, Soup, Meat, Dessert {spoon} Red Wine)

Catering Software Options
(These are all known quantity software companies, but you
should check reviews features and costs to see what works best
for your needs)

1. Pxier – online software for banquet management,
    calendaring, client and contact management, invoice
    tools, event and task organizing, tax help, and marketing
    tools.

2. Knowify – for a smaller catering business, this online
    tool helps with staffing and employee schedules, billing,
    and contract/contact organization. You can control
    what various persons in your business have access to as
    needed

3. Cater Trax – Used in Hospitality, Restaurants, and for
    Caterers this tool has online ordering features, billing
    and invoicing tools, calendaring, customer contact, and a
    number of other tools. It also is exceptional with
    printable reports that but relevant data at your finger
    tips.

4. Better Cater – Recipe costing tools help you with
    budgeting, as well as many of the calendaring and
    invoice features the other programs offer.

Recipe Costing Tool

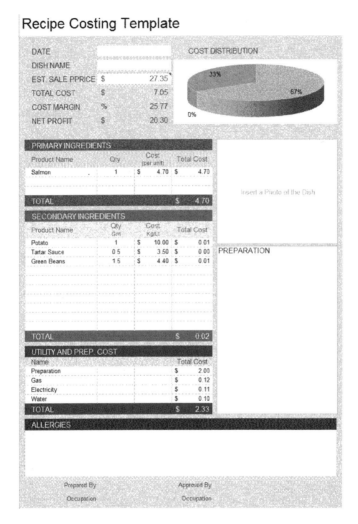

Recipe Costing Template

DATE		COST DISTRIBUTION
DISH NAME		
EST. SALE PPRICE	$ 27.35	
TOTAL COST	$ 7.05	
COST MARGIN	% 25.77	
NET PROFIT	$ 20.30	

PRIMARY INGREDIENTS

Product Name	Qty	Cost (per unit)	Total Cost
Salmon	1	$ 4.70	$ 4.70
TOTAL			**$ 4.70**

SECONDARY INGREDIENTS

Product Name	Qty Gm	Cost Kg/Lt	Total Cost
Potato	1	$ 10.00	$ 0.01
Tartar Sauce	0.5	$ 3.50	$ 0.00
Green Beans	1.5	$ 4.40	$ 0.01
TOTAL			**$ 0.02**

Insert a Photo of the Dish

PREPARATION

UTILITY AND PREP. COST

Name	Total Cost
Preparation	$ 2.00
Gas	$ 0.12
Electricity	$ 0.11
Water	$ 0.10
TOTAL	**$ 2.33**

ALLERGIES

Prepared By	Approved By
Occupation	Occupation

The tool helps you to price menu items based upon quantity, and portion size relative to cost. An example of its deliverable is depicted below. Email products@newbizplaybook.com for your own customizable copy of this tool

41040295R00049

Made in the USA
Middletown, DE
03 April 2019